COLOR-GAMI

Masao Donahue ◇ Eleanor Kwei

THUNDER BAY
P·R·E·S·S

San Diego, California

Thunder Bay Press
An imprint of Printers Row Publishing Group
10350 Barnes Canyon Road, Suite 100
San Diego, CA 92121
www.thunderbaybooks.com

Developed by The Book Shop, Ltd.
Written and edited by Masao Donahue
Box, book, and origami papers designed by Eleanor Kwei

Photography of origami models by Eleanor Kwei and Masao Donahue

Thunder Bay Press
Publisher: Peter Norton
Associate Publisher: Ana Parker
Publishing/Editorial Team: April Farr, Kelly Larsen, Kathryn C. Dalby
Editorial Team: JoAnn Padgett, Melinda Allman, Traci Douglas
Production Team: Jonathan Lopes, Rusty von Dyl

ISBN: 978-1-62686-594-5

Printed in China

22 21 20 19 18   4 5 6 7 8

CONTENTS

Symbols   4

Basic Folds and Bases   5

   Square Base   5

   Bird Base   6

   Blintz Base   8

   Fish Base   9

   Waterbomb Base   10

Lantern   11

Koi   13

Envelope   16

Fox   19

Boat   21

Whale   24

Keepsake Box with Lid   27

Swan   31

Rose   35

Hen and Chicks   38

Tulip   43

Parrot   46

Heart   50

Owl   53

Dress   56

Butterfly   60

Iris   64

Dragonfly   68

Turtle   72

Snail   76

SYMBOLS

---------- Valley fold

— - — - — - Mountain fold

.... Hidden lines reference (usually underneath top layer)

Fold in direction

Fold and unfold in direction

Fold behind

Fold inside

Pleat fold

Crimp fold

⇧ Push or open

↻ Rotate in direction

Turn over

Repeat steps

✂ Cut

• Reference point

⊢—⊣ Spacing reference

Inflate

BASIC FOLDS AND BASES
SQUARE BASE

1 Start with the darker, colored side of the paper facedown.

Valley fold in half in each direction, and unfold. Turn over.

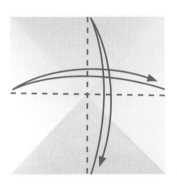

2 Valley fold in half in each direction, and unfold. Turn over. Rotate

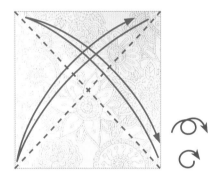

3 Collapse along existing creases, bringing the three tips down toward the bottom.

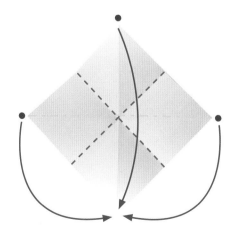

The completed Square Base

BIRD BASE

1 Start with the darker, colored side of the paper facedown.

Complete the Square Base (see page 5) and make sure the opening is pointing down.

2 Valley fold, aligning lower edges to center.

3 Valley fold, wrapping onto flaps from previous step, and unfold.

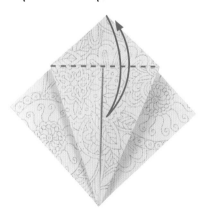

4 Unfold side flaps.

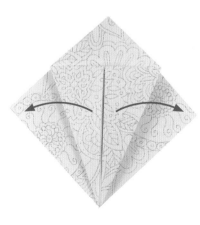

5 Lift top layer and collapse along existing creases.

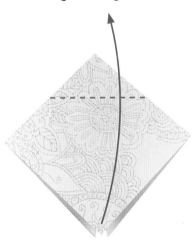

In progress. Top layer is lifted. Bring outer edges of diamond-shape towards the center to complete.

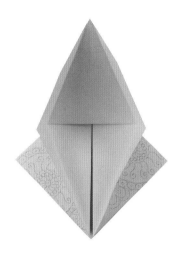

6 Turn over.

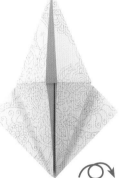

7 Repeat steps 2–6.

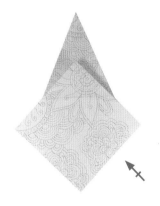

The completed Bird Base

BLINTZ BASE

1 Start with the darker, colored side of the paper facedown.

Valley fold in half in each direction, and unfold.

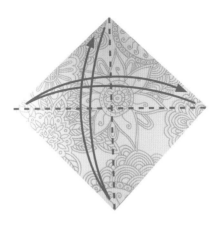

2 Valley fold, aligning tips to center.

The completed Blintz Base

FISH BASE

1 Start with the darker, colored side of the paper facedown.

Valley fold in half in each direction, and unfold.

2 Valley fold, aligning outer edges to center crease, and unfold.

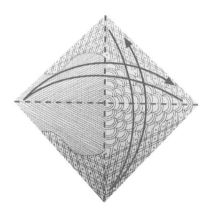

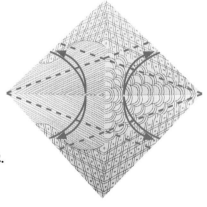

3 Rabbit-ear fold using existing creases. Start with the long, diagonal valley folds which will cause the paper to stand upright, like a rabbit's ear, and then fold that upright section down toward the left. Repeat on bottom half.

The completed Fish Base

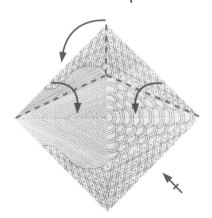

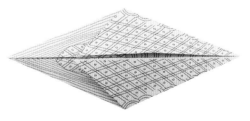

WATERBOMB BASE

1. Start with the darker, colored side facedown.

   Valley fold in half in each direction, and unfold. Turn over.

2. Valley fold in half in each direction, and unfold. Turn over.

3. Collapse along existing creases, bringing the three reference points down toward the bottom.

The completed Waterbomb Base

 # LANTERN

1 Valley fold in half, and unfold.

2 Valley fold, aligning outer edges to center crease.

3 Valley fold corners, leaving a small gap near the middle. See next step for reference. Turn over.

Valley fold between sets of reference points. Turn over.

Valley fold corners, leaving a small gap near the middle. Turn over.

Open the top layers and slightly pull them apart while bringing the lower edge upward to flatten. Repeat on lower section.

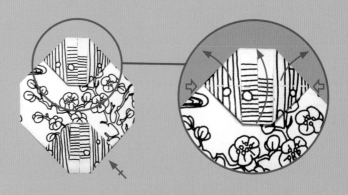

The completed Lantern

KOI

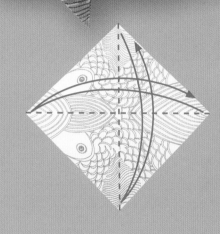

1 Valley fold in half in each direction, and unfold.

2 Valley fold, aligning left edges to center crease.

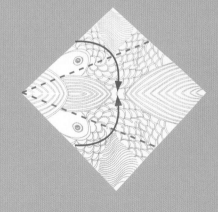

3 Valley fold, aligning right edges to center crease.

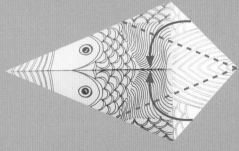

4 Unfold both layers on top section.

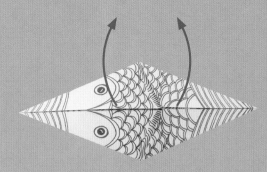

5 Rabbit-ear fold, using existing creases. Start with long diagonal creases, and then lower the raised flap downward to the left.

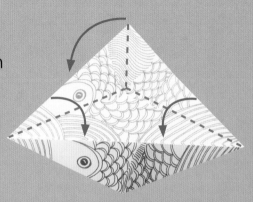

6 Repeat steps 4–5 on lower section. Turn over.

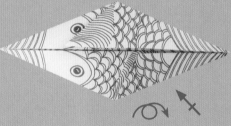

7 Valley fold, aligning tip to the center.

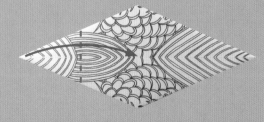

8

Valley fold upward.

9

Valley fold flap in half. Repeat on opposite side.

10

Inside reverse fold, pushing from below to raise the tail. Pre-crease through all layers with a valley fold if necessary.

The completed Koi

ENVELOPE

1 Fold in half horizontally, create pinch marks along sides, and unfold.

2 Fold lower section in half, create pinch marks along sides, and unfold.

3 Valley fold, aligning lower edge to pinch marks from previous step.

4

Valley fold, aligning lower edge to pinch marks from step 1.

5

Valley fold, aligning edges.

6

Valley fold along vertical edges from previous step.

7

Fold in half vertically, create pinch mark along the top edge, and unfold.

8

Valley fold at angle bisectors, using pinch mark from previous step as a guide.

9

Valley fold along horizontal edge, and tuck the point between the layers of the lower section.

The completed Envelope

FOX

1

Make sure the Fox's face on the underside starts out at the right tip.

Valley fold in half horizontally, and unfold. Valley fold in half vertically (but do not unfold).

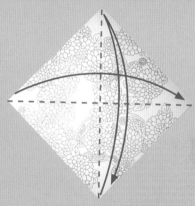

2

Valley fold, aligning top and bottom tips to left corner.

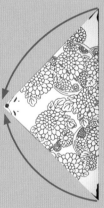

3

Mountain fold in half.

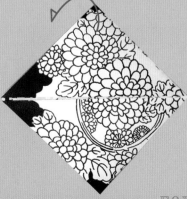

4 Valley fold topmost flap, approximating angle.

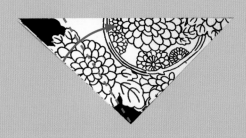

5 Open, and valley fold two layers over onto flap from previous step, and squash fold the face downward. Then valley fold the other end, giving shape to the tail. Rotate.

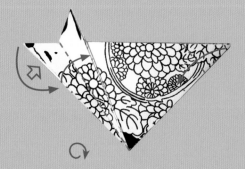

The completed Fox

BOAT

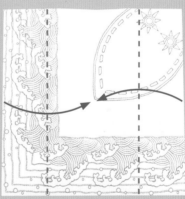

Coloring Tip: Color the darker side of the paper. Start with that side facedown.

1 Valley fold in half, and unfold.

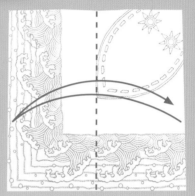

2 Valley fold, aligning outer edges to center crease.

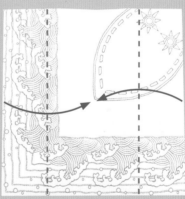

3 Mountain fold in half.

4 Valley fold, aligning corners to center, forming a Blintz Base, and unfold.

5 Lift top layer and shift corners indicated by reference point outward. Establish horizontal crease when edges align along the top edge.

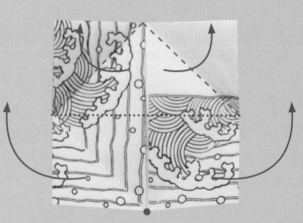

6 Turn over.

7 Repeat steps 4–5.

8

Lift flap.

9

Valley fold square section in half, aligning reference points, while allowing indicated section to flip upward.

10

Valley fold along existing crease.

The completed Boat

WHALE

Coloring Tip: Color the darker side of the paper. Start with that side facedown.

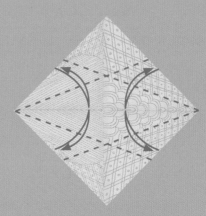

1 Valley fold in half in each direction, and unfold.

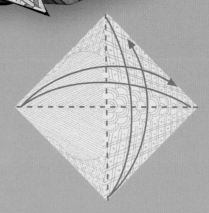

2 Valley fold, aligning outer edges to center crease, and unfold.

3 Rabbit-ear fold using existing creases. Repeat on bottom half.

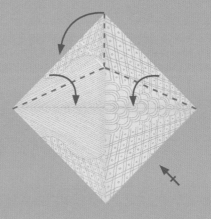

4 Turn over.

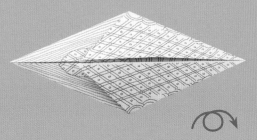

5 Valley fold, aligning left tip to center. Valley fold top and bottom horizontally.

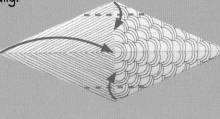

6 Valley fold in half.

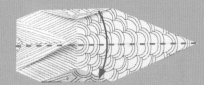

7 Valley fold, pivoting from reference point. Repeat on opposite side.

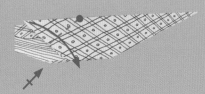

8 Outside reverse fold, approximating the angle. Push from above to wrap the paper over onto itself. First pre-crease through all layers with a valley fold if necessary.

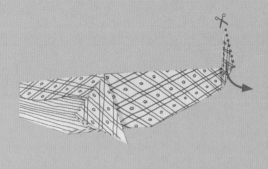

9 Make a small cut, splitting the tail. Valley fold downward at a slight angle.

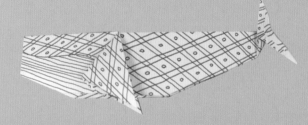

The completed Whale

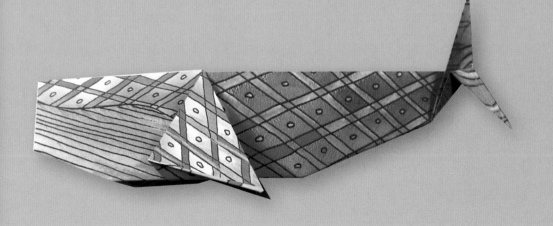

KEEPSAKE BOX WITH LID

The Keepsake Box requires two sheets of paper. Cut roughly ⅛" off two adjacent edges of the second sheet. This will allow the larger lid to sit over the Keepsake Box.

Coloring Tip: Color the darker side of the paper. Start with that side facedown.

1 Valley fold in half in each direction, and unfold.

2 Valley fold, aligning corners to center, forming a Blintz Base.

3 Valley fold, aligning corners to center, forming another Blintz Base.

4 Unfold, reverting back to step 3. Rotate 45 degrees clockwise.

5 Valley fold, aligning top and bottom edges to the center, and unfold.

6 Unfold two flaps.

7 Valley fold, aligning outer edges to the center.

8 Lift side walls from the center while pushing inward where indicated. Paper will collapse in an accordion shape. Then wrap top section around raised walls.

The model will become three dimensional at this point.

In Progress: Side walls are upright. Complete step 8 by wrapping top section around the walls of the keepsake box.

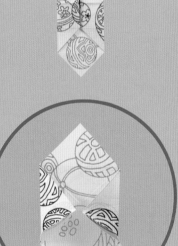

9 Push inward where indicated, then lift and wrap lower flap, forming the final wall.

In Progress: Angled view
showing step 9 in progress.

10

Repeat all steps using
second sheet of paper.

Remember to cut ⅛" off of
two adjacent sides of the
second sheet so that it can
sit inside the slightly larger
lid when folded.

The completed
Keepsake Box with Lid

SWAN

1

Valley fold in half, and unfold.

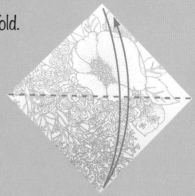

2

Valley fold, aligning left edges to center crease. Turn over.

3

Valley fold, aligning long edges to center crease.

4 Valley fold in half.

5 Valley fold, giving shape to the beak.

6 Mountain fold in half.

7 Lift the neck, and then flatten when you have found a suitable angle.

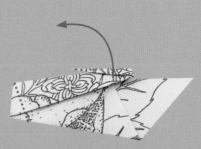

8 Inside reverse fold, bringing upper corner down toward the lower corner. Pre-crease if necessary.

9 Inside reverse fold hidden flap so that the tail protrudes slightly, keeping the lower diagonal edges aligned.

10 Lift the head, and flatten when you have found a suitable angle.

11 Inside reverse fold to shorten the beak slightly.

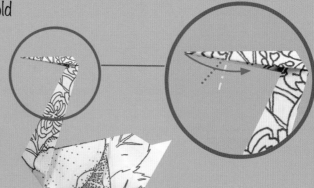

12

Inside reverse fold again, pointing the beak downward.

13

Inside reverse fold one final time, redirecting the beak.

The completed Swan

ROSE

1 Valley fold in half in each direction, and unfold.

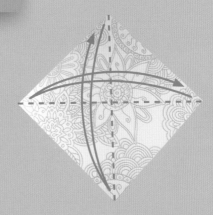

2 Valley fold, aligning tips to center, forming a Blintz Base.

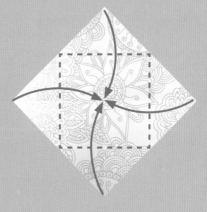

3 Valley fold, aligning tips to center, forming another Blintz Base.

4 Valley fold, aligning tips to center, forming a third Blintz Base. Turn over.

5 Valley fold, aligning tips to center, forming a final Blintz Base. Crease as firmly as possible. Turn over.

6 Valley fold four quadrants at slight angles.

7 Valley fold four sections of underside layers below at slight angles.

8 Turn over.

9 Valley fold four flaps so that tips protrude beyond edges.

10 Turn over.

The completed Rose

HEN and CHICKS

1 Valley fold in half in each direction, and unfold.

2 Valley fold, aligning left tip to center.

After folding, color the blank triangular section that appears. This is the Hen's comb. Turn over.

3 Valley fold, aligning left edge to center crease.

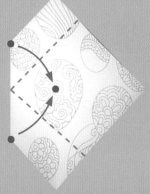

 Pleat fold by folding diamond-shaped section in half and then folding the folded flap back in the opposite direction. Make sure tip protrudes slightly beyond the edge.

 Pivot from reference point, shifting edge slightly, then flatten. Repeat on lower section.

6 Valley fold in half.

 Inside reverse fold. If necessary, before attempting the reverse fold, pre-crease by valley folding diagonally, and unfold. Then use those creases to reverse fold.

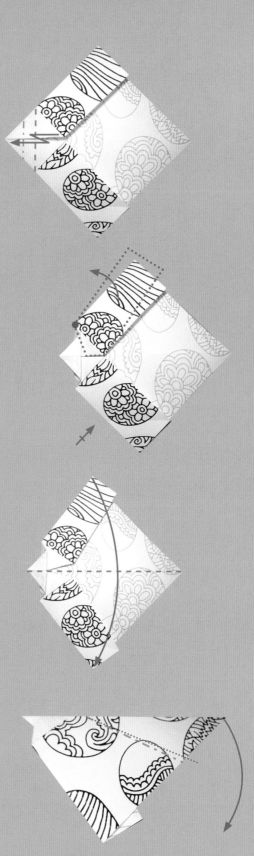

8 Inside reverse fold once more, giving shape to the tail.

9 Mountain fold inward, establishing the base of the model. Repeat on opposite side.

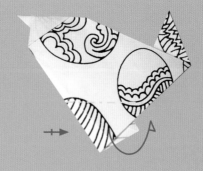

10 Raise the comb by opening the model partially, and shifting the outer layer on both sides. Turn over.

Note: If the beak disappears when the comb is raised, adjust the interior layers until it reappears.

The completed Hen

The Chicks are folded using 3" x 3" paper. Cut along the dotted lines of the larger, 6" x 6" sheet before folding.

Coloring Tip: After cutting the paper down to 3" x 3" pieces, color the darker sides and orient them as shown (left). Start with the colored sides faceup.

1 To fold the Chicks, first orient either paper above as shown. Valley fold in half in each direction, and unfold. Turn over.

2 Valley fold, aligning left corners to center.

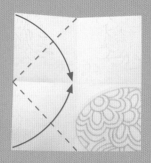

3 Valley fold vertically at roughly the one-third mark of right side. Then pleat fold the left side, forming the beak.

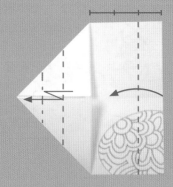

4 Valley fold in half.

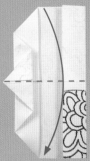

5

Inside reverse fold.

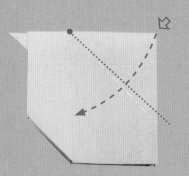

6

Mountain fold inside the model, starting from the indicated corner. Repeat on the opposite side. Turn over.

Repeat all steps using second sheet of paper but do not turn it over on the final step. Use different edges to position the chicks (as shown below).

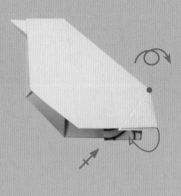

The completed Chicks

The completed Hen and Chicks

TULIP

Coloring Tip: Color the darker side of the paper. Start with that side facedown.

1 Orient the paper as shown and refer to page 10 to fold into a Waterbomb Base.

2 Valley fold top flaps, aligning outer tips to top.

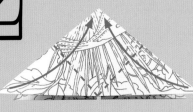

3 Repeat step 2 on opposite side.

4 Fold one flap over on the front and back of the model.

5

Valley fold, aligning upper-right edge slightly beyond the vertical center.

6

Mirror previous step, overlapping onto flap.

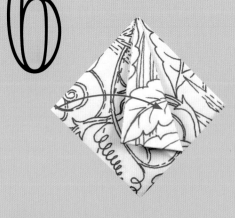

7

Turn over.

8

Repeat steps 5–6.

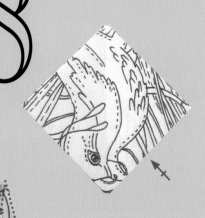

9

Tuck left flap between the layers of the right flap. Curl the bottom edge when the flaps are connected, making the model three-dimensional. Repeat on opposite side.

10

Inflate by blowing air into the hole at the bottom.

Seen from below

11

Carefully curl the four petals, making sure that the flaps from step 9 remain in place.

The completed Tulip

PARROT

Coloring Tip:
Color the darker side of the paper. Start with that side faceup.

1 Orient the paper as shown.
Turn over.

2 Refer to page 9 to fold into
a Fish Base.

3 Unfold bottom section.
Turn over.

4 Rabbit-ear fold, pointing the
ear to the left.

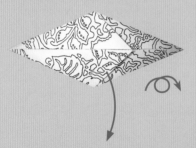

5 Turn over.

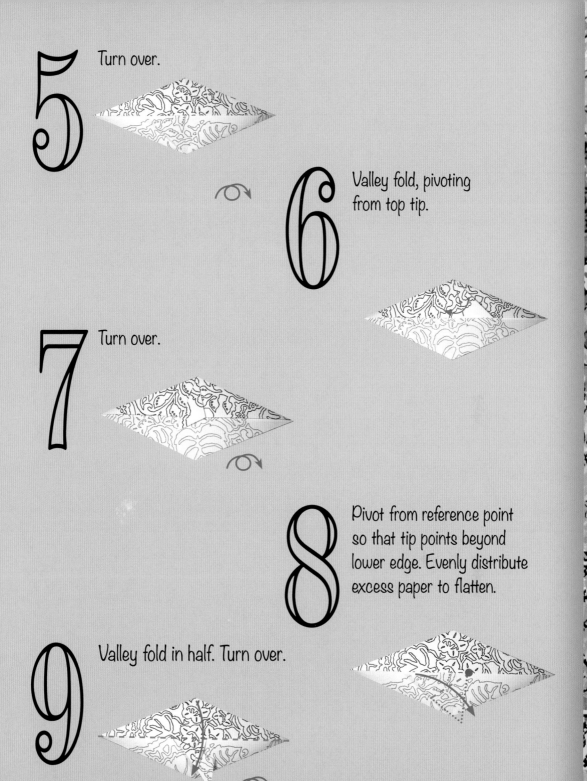

6 Valley fold, pivoting from top tip.

7 Turn over.

8 Pivot from reference point so that tip points beyond lower edge. Evenly distribute excess paper to flatten.

9 Valley fold in half. Turn over.

10

Valley fold, approximating
the angle, and unfold.

11

Valley fold between ends of
existing creases. Rotate.

12

Open top layer and shift it
to the left, then lower the
beak to the right.

13

Turn over.

14

Valley fold section at angle bisector.

15

Valley fold top layer downward.

16

Valley fold tail.

The completed Parrot

HEART

1 Valley fold in half in each direction, create pinch marks, and unfold.

2 Valley fold, aligning top and bottom edges to center, and unfold.

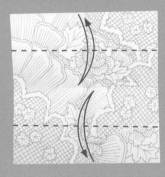

3 Fold, aligning top and bottom edges to creases on opposite sides, create pinch marks, and unfold.

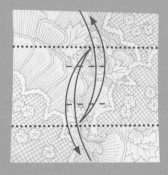

4 Valley fold, aligning top and bottom edges to center.

5 Valley fold in half. Rotate 90-degrees so that opening faces down.

6 Valley fold, aligning edges to pinch marks, and unfold.

7 Inside reverse fold at angle bisectors. Pre-crease if necessary.

8 Inside reverse fold both upper corners. Valley fold lower layers at angle bisectors, and unfold.

9

Push downward carefully, giving shape to the top of the heart. Reinforce creases if necessary.

The model will become three dimensional at this point.

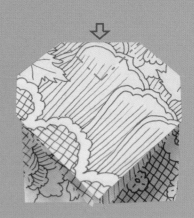

10

Tuck the lower section between the layers of the top section. The creases from step 8 will help.

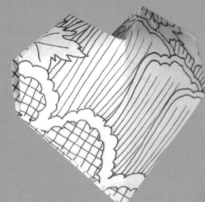

The completed Heart

OWL

Coloring Tip: Color the darker side of the paper. Start with that side facedown.

1 Orient the paper as shown and refer to page 5 to fold into a Square Base, and then proceed to pages 6–7 to fold it into a Bird Base.

2 Lower flaps on both sides.

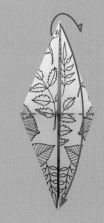

3 Valley fold, aligning top edges to center crease. Repeat on opposite side.

4 Lift center flap, pivoting from reference point, and flatten when edges align. See next photo for reference. Repeat on opposite side.

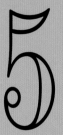

In Progress: The wing is curled here to avoid unnecessary creasing. Three reference points mark aligned edges.

5 Valley fold, lowering tip beyond diagonal edges.

6 Pleat fold, tucking a small section underneath triangular flap, giving shape to the beak. Turn over.

7 Cut carefully through the top flap, as indicated, then raise freed flaps, giving shape to the ears. Turn over.

8 Cut carefully through the top flap, as indicated, then pivot freed flaps, giving shape to the feet.

The completed Owl

DRESS

1 Valley fold in half, and unfold. Turn over.

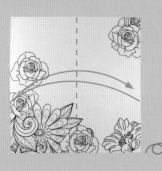

2 Valley fold, aligning outer edges to center crease, and unfold. Turn over.

3 Raise along creases from previous step, and align those to center, completing the Pleat Folds.

4 Turn over.

5 Valley fold upward, leaving roughly ¾" from the top edge.

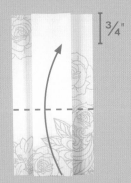

¾"

6 Turn over.

7 Valley fold downward, roughly ¾" from bottom edge.

¾"

8 Rotate. Turn over.

9 Pivot from reference point, shift top layer until it meets the bottom corner of the lower layer, and flatten. Repeat on opposite side.

10 Valley fold, aligning top edges to vertical edge of layers underneath, and unfold.

11 Turn over.

12 Valley fold top layer downward, evenly squash folding the raised triangular sections on both sides.

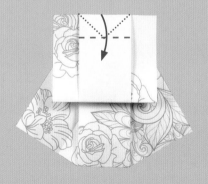

In Progress: When top layer is lowered, triangular sections will rise. Flatten them evenly.

13

Valley fold, wrapping top layer of upper section around vertical edge. When that is complete, valley fold lower section of dress, keeping the lower edge aligned. Repeat on the opposite side.

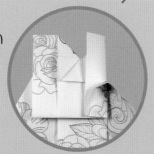

In Progress: Allow the section highlighted with the reference point to curl, while the long rectangular section above is being creased.

14

Valley fold between sets of reference points. Turn over.

The completed Dress

BUTTERFLY

Coloring Tip: Color the darker side of the paper. Start with that side faceup.

1 Valley fold in half in each direction, and unfold. Turn over.

2 Valley fold, aligning corners to center, forming a Blintz Base.

3 Turn over.

4 Valley fold, aligning tips to center, forming another Blintz Base, and unfold. Turn over.

5 Unfold entirely.

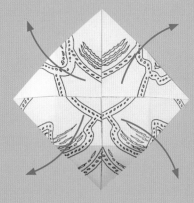

6 Valley fold, aligning outer edges to center.

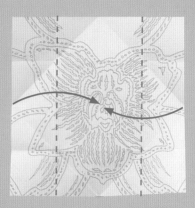

7 Valley fold top layer along diagonal creases, causing the corners to flip outward, and lower raised section along existing crease.

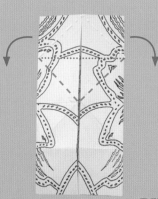

8 Repeat step 7 on lower section.

9 Mountain fold in half.

10 Valley fold, lowering top flaps.

11 Valley fold between sets of reference points.

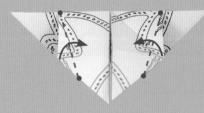

12

Valley fold in half.

13

Fold in opposite direction, pivoting from reference point. Repeat on opposite side.

14

Flip top flap to opposite side.

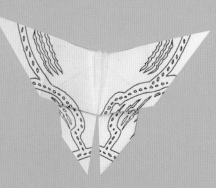

The completed Butterfly

IRIS

1 Orient the paper as shown and refer to page 5 to fold into a Square Base. Finish by rotating so that the opening points upward.

2 Valley fold, aligning lower edges to center crease, and unfold. Repeat on opposite side.

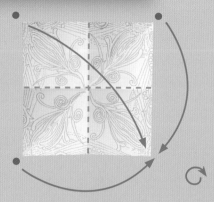

3 Lift flap, open between layers, and squash fold.

4 Repeat step 3 on remaining three sides.

5 Valley fold, aligning upper edges to center, and unfold.

6 Valley fold in half, and unfold.

7 Lift top layer along horizontal crease, and draw raised edges to center.

8   Repeat steps 5–7 on remaining three sides.

9   Valley fold, raising flap. Repeat on remaining three sides.

10   Valley fold, aligning lower edges to center.

11   Repeat step 10 on remaining three sides.

12

Fold one flap over to the opposite side on the front and back.

13

Carefully curl the four petals.

The completed Iris

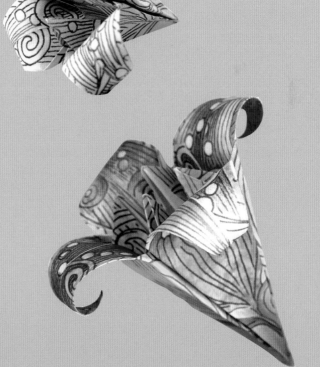

DRAGONFLY

Coloring Tip: Color the darker side of the paper. Start with that side facedown.

1 Orient the paper as shown and refer to page 5 to fold into a Square Base, and then proceed to pages 6-7 to fold it into a Bird Base.

2 Lower flap on back.

3 Valley fold, aligning flap's edges to center crease, and unfold.

4 Push lower flaps upward, and tuck behind the top section, similar to a pleat fold.

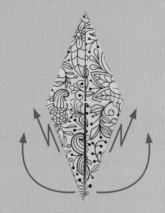

5 Valley fold top triangular section at angle bisector. Towards the bottom of the crease, paper will protrude upward; carefully shift the paper so that it can flatten. Repeat on opposite side.

6 Turn over.

7 Valley fold lower section at angle bisector. Towards the top of the crease, paper will protrude upward; carefully shift the paper so that it can flatten. Repeat on opposite side.

8 Mountain fold in half. Rotate.

9 Outside reverse fold. Push from below, where indicated, to redirect the head.

10 Perform consecutive reverse folds starting from the tip, shortening the head. Leave roughly ¾" remaining.

11 Crimp fold by pivoting from the reference point, establishing a set of creases on both sides of the model.

12

Valley fold the tip of the wing. Repeat on opposite side.

13

Cut the wings in half until meeting the top of the body. Then lower all four wings. View from above.

The completed Dragonfly

TURTLE

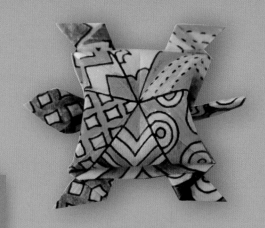

Coloring Tip: Color the darker side of the paper. Start with that side facedown.

1 Orient the paper as shown and refer to page 10 to fold into a Waterbomb Base.

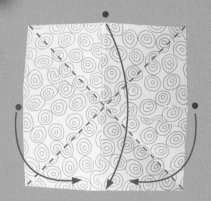

2 Valley fold, aligning outer tips to top, and unfold.

3 Valley fold, aligning top to baseline, and unfold.

4 Lift top layer, and collapse by squash folding the sides.

5 Valley fold top flap, aligning tip to paper's edge underneath layer.

6 Lift top layer, align bottom corners to top, and collapse sides along existing creases.

7 Turn over.

8 Repeat steps 2–7.

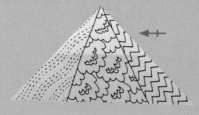

9 Valley fold both sides.

10 Valley fold, leaving a small gap at the bottom.

11 Turn over. Repeat steps 9–10 on opposite side.

12 Inside reverse fold.

13 Insert fingers between layers created in step 5 on both sides and carefully pry model open. View from above.

14 Flatten head.

The completed Turtle

SNAIL

Coloring Tip: Color the darker side of the paper. Start with that side facedown.

1 Orient the paper as shown and refer to page 5 to fold into a Square Base. Finish by rotating so that the opening points upward.

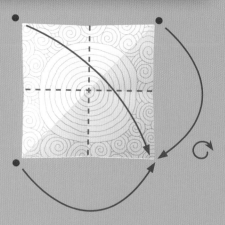

2 Valley fold, aligning lower edges to center crease, and unfold. Repeat on opposite side.

3 Lift flap, separate layers, and squash fold.

Repeat step 3 on remaining three flaps.

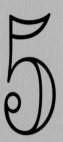

Valley fold left side at angle bisector. Valley fold right side at roughly one-third mark.

Valley fold right side at angle bisector.

Valley fold left side at angle bisector.

8 Fold two flaps over to the right.

9 Repeat steps 5–8 on remaining three sides.

10 Valley fold one flap over on both sides.

11 Inside reverse fold underside flaps on both sides, angling the antennae to your liking.

12

Fold tip inside the model.
Repeat on opposite side.

13

Valley fold model in half,
creasing firmly, and unfold.

14

Lift along crease from previous
step so that the lower half
stands perpendicular.
View from the side.

15

Side view. Begin separating
layers by lightly pulling adjacent
flaps downward, starting near
the base. This will cause
the shell to balloon and
become rounder.

In Progress: Side view. Shell begins to take shape. Continue by gently pulling edges downward.

In Progress: For final shaping, gently pull opposite ends from the base of the model, allowing the shell to become rounder at the top.

The completed Snail